# Dedication

To Eric & Avery — For inspiring and believing in this dream and giving me the opportunity to chase it! I love you both dearly! —J.A.

To all my students just starting out their careers — Keep moving forward even when there are obstacles. You can make it! —C.W.

YOUNG AT HEART
PUBLISHING

Copyright © 2021 by Jodi Adams
Illustrations by Christina Wald

**Special Thanks To**
**Sarah Fabiny — Editor**
**Christina Wald — Illustrator**
**David Miles — Book Designer**
**Doug & Kelly Adams — Producers**
**Tom & Barb Monahan — Producers**
**Carol Johannesen — Producer**
**Kickstarter & Indiegogo Supporters — Producers**

All rights reserved. No part of this book may be reproduced or transmitted in any form or by any means, electronic or mechanical, including photocopying, recording, or by any information storage and retrieval system, without written permission from the author.

978-1-7348366-0-8 (Hardcover)
978-1-7348366-1-5 (Paperback)
978-1-7348366-2-2 (eBook)

# THE TRAIN ROLLS ON

JODI ADAMS

ILLUSTRATED BY
CHRISTINA WALD

Here comes the next train!
It's got work to do—
passengers await
a ride to the zoo.

There's NO time to waste.
They must depart soon.
The zoo's grand opening
is THIS afternoon!

Each ticket is checked and given a punch. The passengers board— they're one eager bunch!

Each animal's ready.
The crew is set, too.
The engineer waves.
Next stop: the **ZOO!**

The coal has been poured,
so welcome aboard...

## AND THE TRAIN ROLLS ON!
chugga chugga choo choo!

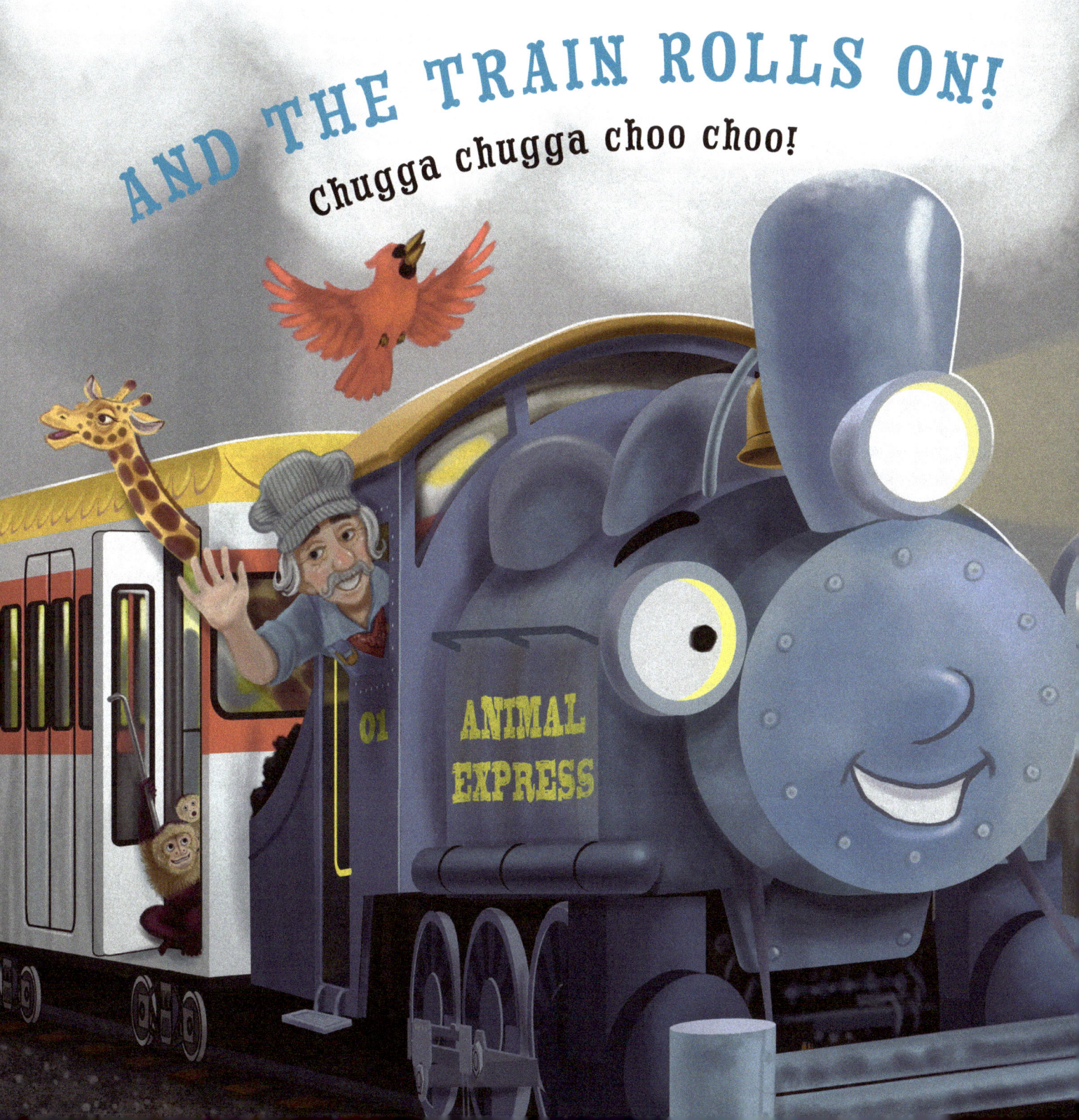

Not far down the track,
the train meets a hill
so tall and so steep
it tests the train's will.

The train inches upward
and comes to a stop...
then gives one last push
and reaches the top!

The train's rather spent from its mighty ascent...

## BUT THE TRAIN ROLLS ON!

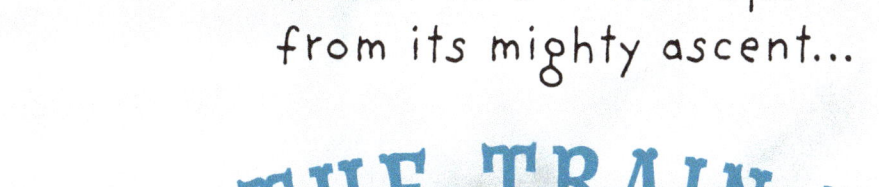

The train calmly chugs
along a steep ridge.
It comes to a river
and tall, narrow bridge.

The train cars all tremble.
Their wheels slow a bit,
but the engine digs deep
and refuses to quit.

The train is afraid
but won't be delayed...

The animals become more cramped and less cozy. The monkeys get restless. The elephant gets nosy.

The lion gets angry.
The giraffe tries to stand.
Things escalate quickly.
They're soon out of hand!

The train fights the riot
until it grows quiet...

## THEN THE TRAIN ROLLS ON!

chugga chugga choo choo!

The train hums along—
click clickety clack,
and everything seems
to be back on track.

Then it comes 'round a bend,
and what does it see?
There's something ahead...

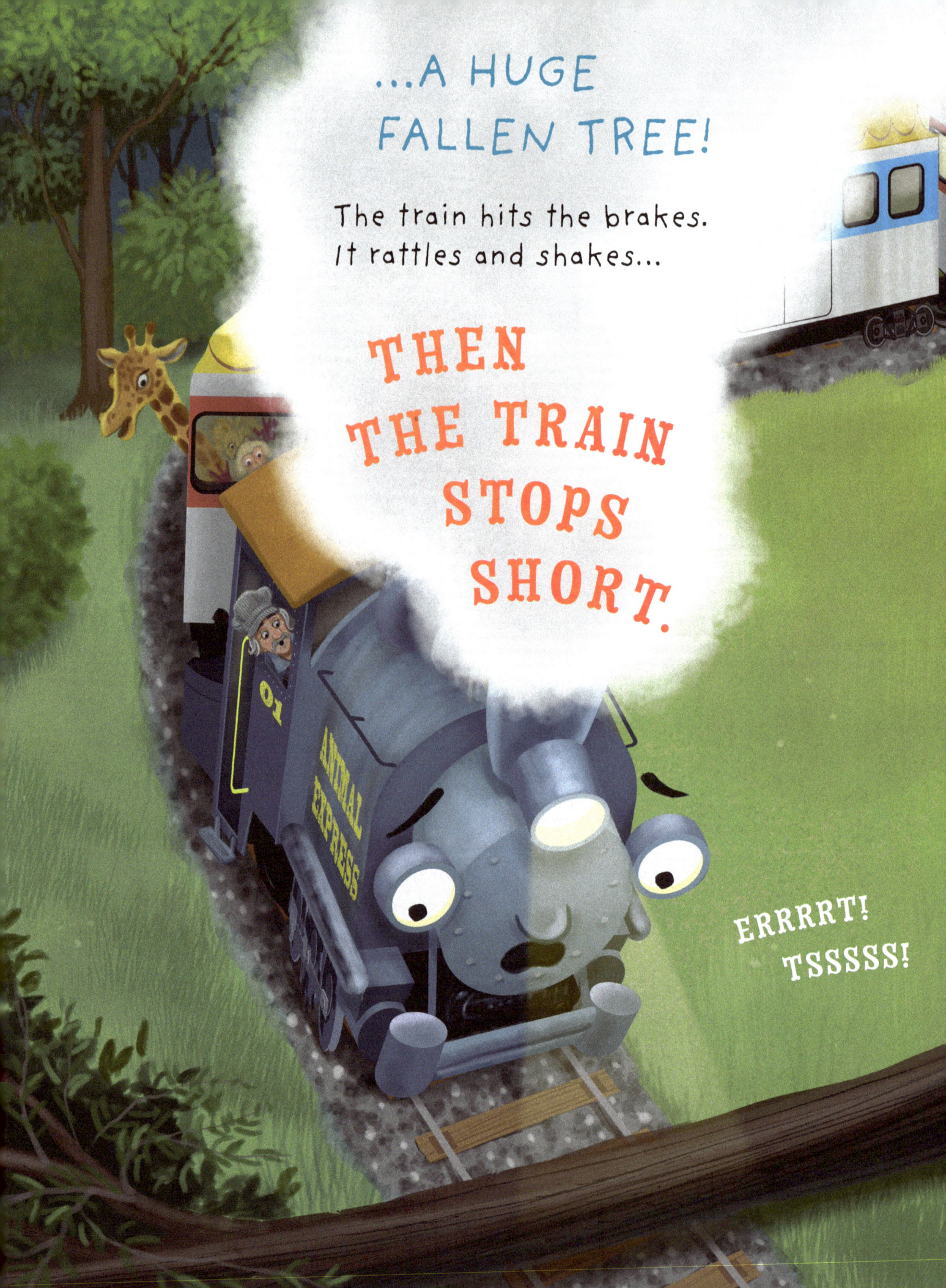

The engineer sighs
and examines the tree.
Oh, what will they do?
The event starts at three!

Concerned they won't make it,
he picks up the phone,
but nobody answers.
The train's on its own!

With nothing close by
and the zoo still so far,
he does the unthinkable...

Each offers a trait that makes the team great...

...AND THE TRAIN ROLLS ON!

Here comes the proud train!
There's still work to do—
it races the clock
to get to the zoo.

It finally arrives—
not a moment to spare.
Upon its approach,
loud cheers fill the air.

The crowd celebrates.
A party awaits...

As passengers unload,
the engineer descends.
He smiles and winks
and thanks his new friends.

Then he hops in the engine
and bids them adieu.
He readies the train
and signals the crew.

The animals say
"What a **wild** day!"

# Glossary

Some of the words in this book may be new to your child. Expand your child's vocabulary by familiarizing them with any new words and helping them to understand their meanings.

**Ascent** – climb
**Bid adieu** – say goodbye
**Debut** – first appearance
**Delayed** – late or slowed down
**Depart** – leave
**Descends** – comes down from
**Eager** – excited
**Examines** – looks closely at
**Restless** – antsy or fidgety
**Riot** – disturbance or unrest
**Spent** – tired or exhausted
**Trait** – feature
**Tremble** – shake or shiver
**Unthinkable** – crazy or ridiculous
**Escalate** – worsen
**Will** – drive or motivation

## Meet the Author

Jodi Adams is a former Crime Scene Investigator turned stay-at-home mom and children's book author. Jodi has always loved reading and writing, but it wasn't until her daughter was born that she rediscovered her love of children's fiction and decided to write and publish stories of her own.

When she is not reading or writing, Jodi loves to cook and bake (mostly eat!), run, golf, play sand volleyball, and spend time with her family. She grew up in Iowa but now lives in Omaha, NE, with her husband, Eric, and her daughter, Avery. You can find out more about Jodi and her books at www.jodiadamsauthor.com.

## Meet the Illustrator

Christina Wald is a professional children's book illustrator specializing in animal and science work. A prolific artist with over 20 years of experience in the field, she has worked with numerous major publishers and on many smaller-scale projects directly with authors.

Christina holds a BS in Industrial Design from the University of Cincinnati and loves to combine her two passions: travel and illustration. She lives in Cincinnati with her husband—a toy engineer—and three cats. You can find out more about Christina and view more of her artwork at www.christinawald.com.

## Thank you for buying my book!

I sincerely hope that you enjoyed reading *The Train Rolls On* and that it inspires you and your children to persevere through life's many challenges!

If you feel that this book and its message positively impact kids' lives, here are the best ways to pay it forward:

1. Tell your friends
2. Tell me at www.jodiadamsauthor.com/contact
3. Leave an honest review on Amazon (or other retailer)

Reviews are powerful for authors like me. They help others learn about my book and decide if it's right for them. I really appreciate your time and energy. Thank you for your support!!!

—Jodi

---

### Free Activities & Coloring Pages:
www.jodiadamsauthor.com/resources

### Connect:
Instagram.com/jadams_author

Facebook.com/jodi.adams.14418

Sign-up for my monthly newsletter at www.jodiadamsauthor.com and receive a free gift!

CPSIA information can be obtained
at www.ICGtesting.com
Printed in the USA
BVHW020925170822
644791BV00005B/65

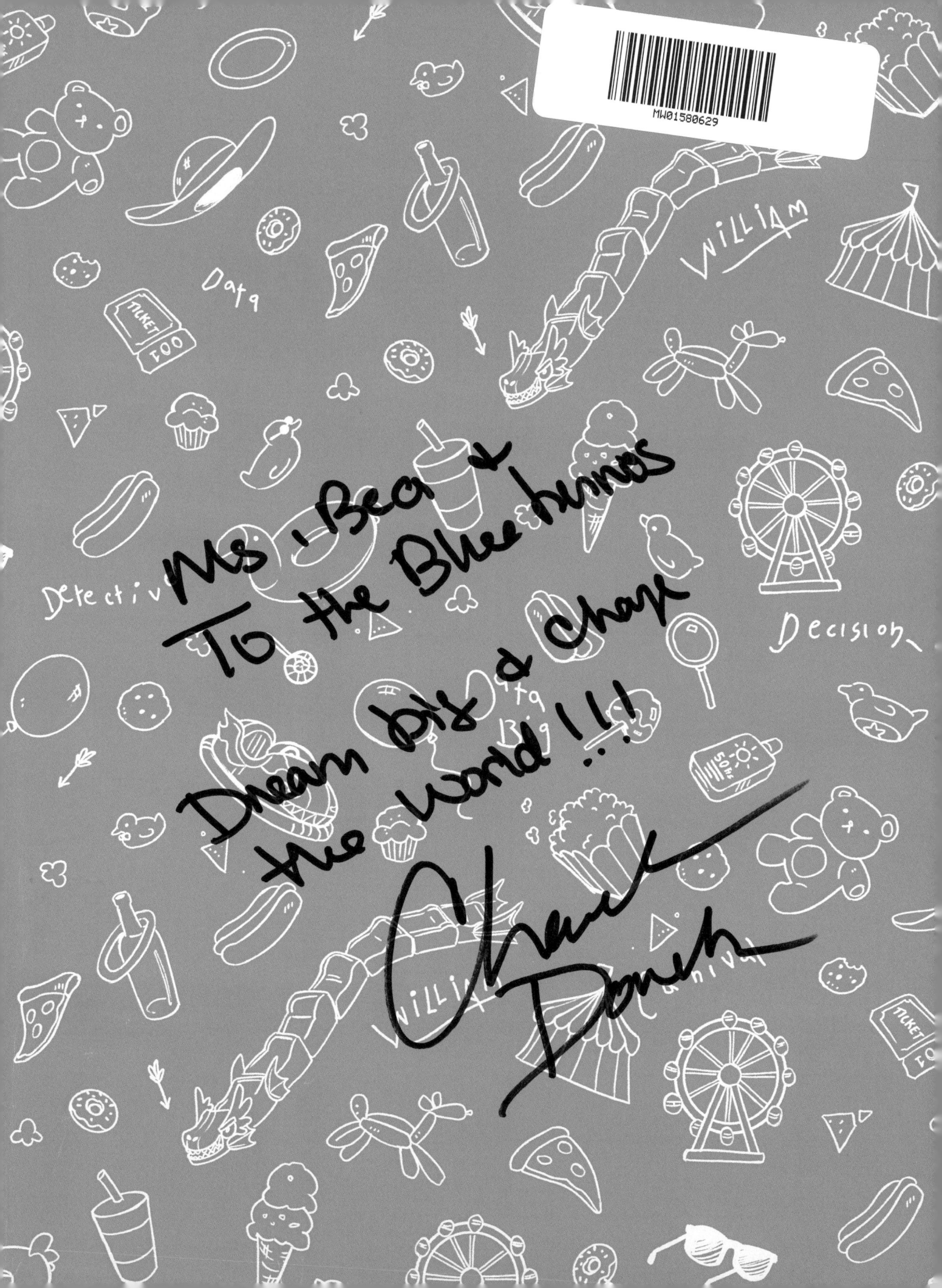

Ms. Bea +
To the Blue hinos
Dream big & Chay
the World!!!

Chuck Donch

115 Linda Vista
Sedona, AZ 86336 USA
https://www.TechnicsPub.com

Edited by Jamie Hoberman
Cover design and illustrations by Mariam Trejo

All rights reserved. No part of this book may be reproduced or transmitted in any form or by any means, electronic or mechanical, including photocopying, recording or by any information storage and retrieval system, without written permission from the publisher, except for brief quotations in a review.

The authors and publisher have taken care in the preparation of this book, but make no expressed or implied warranty of any kind and assume no responsibility for errors or omissions. No liability is assumed for incidental or consequential damages in connection with or arising out of the use of the information or programs contained herein.

All trade and product names are trademarks, registered trademarks, or service marks of their respective companies and are the property of their respective holders and should be treated as such. LEGO® is a trademark of the LEGO Group of companies which does not sponsor, authorize, or endorse this book. This book is not an official Minecraft product or partner. Not approved by or associated with Mojang or Microsoft.

First Printing 2024

Copyright © 2024 by Chandra Donelson

ISBN, print ed. 9781634626187
ISBN, Kindle ed. 9781634626194
ISBN, PDF ed. 9781634626217

Library of Congress number 2024940211

Chandra Donelson & Jordan Morrow
Illustrated by Mariam Trejo

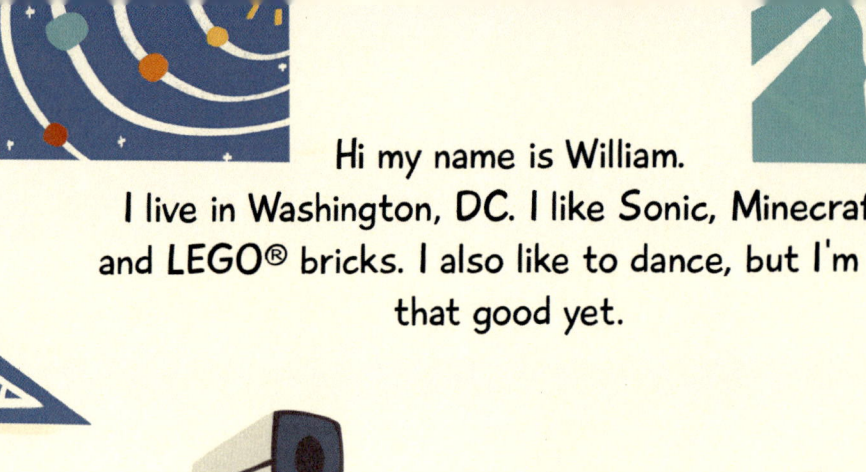

Hi my name is William.
I live in Washington, DC. I like Sonic, Minecraft, and LEGO® bricks. I also like to dance, but I'm not that good yet.

Data is a collection of information that helps us learn and understand more about the world around us. Data is collected by observing what you see, hear, touch, smell, or taste.

It might not be obvious at first, but Mommy says everyone uses data.

**Police** use data to fight crime.

**Athletes** use data to help them win trophies.

**Santa** even uses data to create the naughty or nice list!

Today is an exciting day because I am going on a special mission, and you'll be coming with me! When we finish this mission, we will get our first data detective certificate and badge.
Are you ready? Let's go!

"Mommy, who is konk-ka-tay-tive and clock-a-tay-tive? Are they secret agents?" I ask. "Konk-ka-tay-tive and clock-a-tay-tive?" she says with a confused look.

"Yesterday, I heard you talking about them," I explain. "They were going to help you solve a problem, but it was going to be really hard."

"Are you kidding me? There are different types of data?" I ask. "Yes," Mommy says. "Quantitative data is about numbers and measurements, like how many or how much."

Qualitative data is about descriptions and observations, like what something looks, feels, smells, sounds, or tastes like." Confused, I ask, "Can you show me what you mean?"

"WOW! You're a cookie-counting rockstar!" Mommy says, clapping her hands. "Thats quantitative data because you counted how many cookies I made."

## Operation: Collect that Data

Let's collect quantitative data.
Can you help William count other items in the kitchen?

Then, Mommy hands me the most delicious-looking cookie in the world and asks me to tell her about it. I can't wait to try it, so I take a really big bite. "Mmm, it's so yummy! It's brown, soft, and filled with chocolate chips!"

"You're right! That's qualitative data because you are describing the cookie," Mommy says.

## Operation: Collect that Data

Let's collect qualitative data. Can you help William describe other items in the kitchen?

"Oh, I get it now!" I say. "It's actually just counting and describing. So why do they have really big names?" I ask.

Mommy leans in and whispers, "Shhh, those are secret code words that only data detectives know." Wow! I can't wait to be a data detective and learn more code words.

**KNOCK KNOCK**
Hmmm! Who's at the door? I run to the door.
"Hey, Mommy, it's Luca!!!" I shout. Luca is my best friend.
He is the same age as me and speaks two languages.

"Are you ready to go on a mission?" I ask.
"Yes, I am ready," Luca says, "but where are we going?"
"It's a surprise," I yell. Do you know?

## Operation: Collect that Data

Let's collect qualitative data.
Can you observe the items in the living room to guess where the mission is?

You're right!
Our mission is at the carnival!

When we arrive at the ticket booth, I feel even more excited. The rides are big with bright colors, and the music makes me feel super happy. I can't wait to start our fun mission and earn a special badge!

"Race you to the Ferris wheel!" I say to Luca, and we both run towards the ride.

When we arrive, the line is a gazillion miles long, and I start feeling a little scared.

My fingers keep fidgeting, and I can't stop bouncing on my toes, which makes Luca laugh. Just as my tummy starts to feel butterflies and my teeth begin to chatter, Mommy leans in and whispers

Are you ready for your first mission?

YOU BETCHA!

"Can you tell me how many people are in line for the Ferris wheel?" Mommy asks. Excitedly, we go to the front of the line and count every person waiting. "1, 2, 3, 4, 5 … 95, 96, 97, 98, 99, 100. There are 100 people!"

"You are amazing! That's quantitative data because you counted how many people you see," Mommy says. Hearing those words makes me really happy. I take out my special notebook and write down the number of people in the line.

# Operation: Collect that Data

Let's collect quantitative data. Can you help William count the people in the line wearing your favorite color shirt?

After waiting for 76 thousand hours, it is finally our turn to ride the Ferris wheel. We quickly get into our cart, and Mommy gives us our next mission. "Can you find and describe all the wacky things you see?" she says. Excitedly, I use my special binoculars to help me see better. I find a pig serving ice cream, a table made out of a pizza box, and a monster truck with donut wheels. The higher we go, the more wacky things I see! "I did it, Mom!" I yell.

"Great job! That's qualitative data because you described the wacky things you see," Mommy explains.

# Operation: Collect that Data

Let's collect qualitative data.
What other wacky things do you see?

After the Ferris wheel, we race to the balloon dart booth. "Let's pop some balloons!" Luca says. "Pop, pop, pop," I yell. Luca and I grab the darts from the counter, and Mommy gives us our next mission. "Can you tell me how many balloons you see?" Mommy asks.

"1, 2, 3, 4, 5 … 21, 22, 23, 24, 25. There are 25 balloons!" "That's fantastic! You collected quantitative data by counting the balloons!" Mommy says. I feel happy to hear Mommy say I did a good job. I take out my special notebook and write down the number of balloons in the booth.

# Operation: Collect that Data

Let's collect quantitative data. Can you help William count all of the polka dot balloons?

After we finish counting the balloons, Mommy gives us our next mission. "Now, I want you to pop the balloons, and then describe how they look," she says.

Luca pops a green balloon and says, "ONE! It's green like slime!"

I pop a red balloon and say "Two! It's red like a juicy watermelon!"

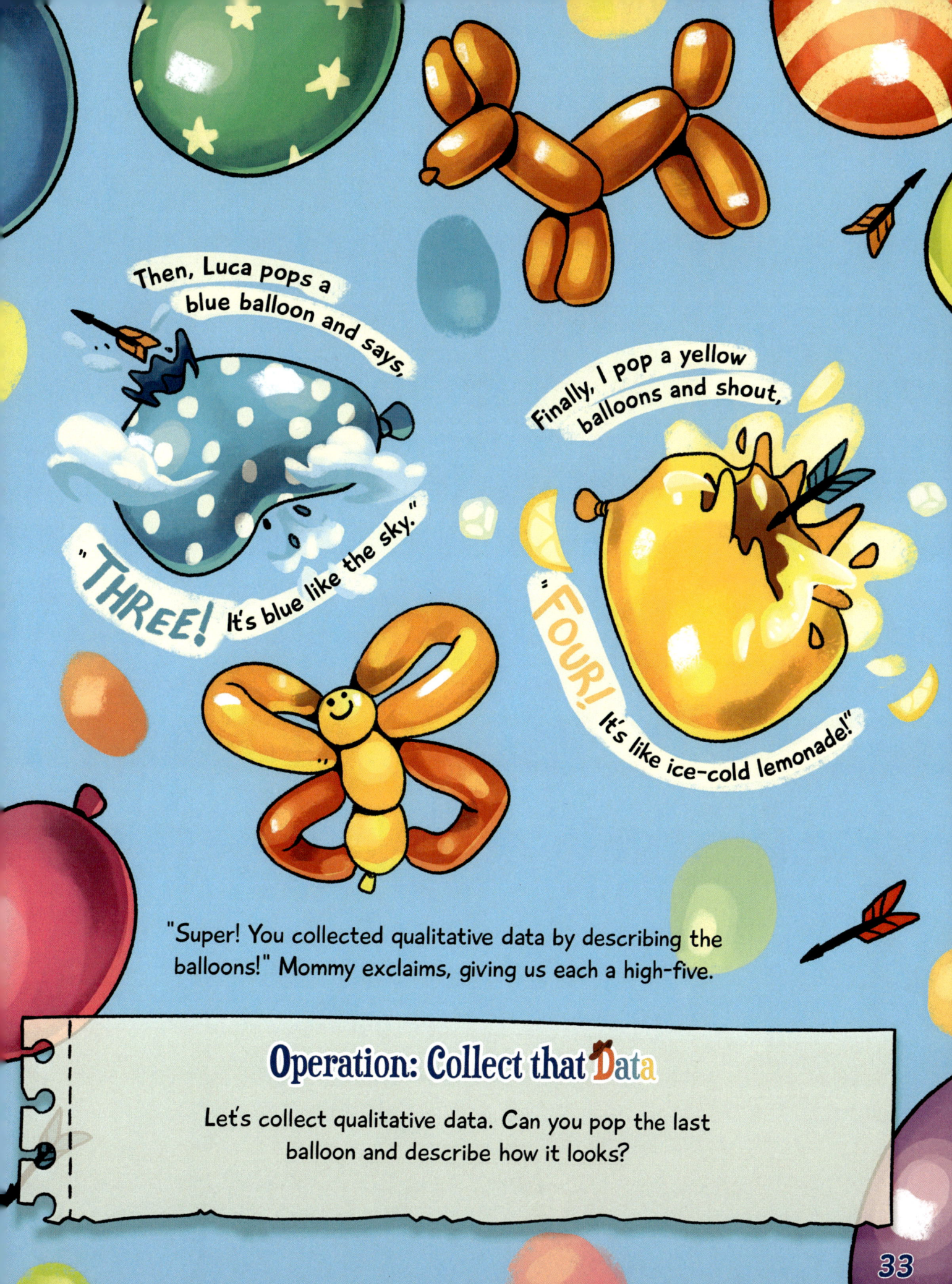

We are so excited that we want to try more rides and games to collect more data. But we need your help! Can you help us make a decision?

## Operation: Collect that Data

Let's make a decision. Where should William go?

page 36      page 38      page 40      page 42

First, we go on the roller coaster. We count the number of loops, describe how fast it goes, and how it makes us feel.

## Operation: Collect that Data

Let's collect quantitative and qualitative data. Can you count the number of kids on the rollercoaster? Can you describe how the other kids on the roller coaster feel?

Then, we go to the ring toss booth. We count how many rings we throw and how many land on the bottles. We also talk about the colors of the rings and the sound they make when they land.

## Operation: Collect that Data

Let's collect quantitative and qualitative data. Can you count the number of rings that William and Luca have on the bottles? Who has more? Can you describe the wacky things you see?

Next, we go to the bumper cars.
We count how many times we bump into other cars and describe how it feels when we bump.

# Operation: Collect that Data

Let's collect quantitative and qualitative data.
Can you count the number of kids that look happy?
Can you describe how the bumper cars look?

Then, we play the Lucky Duck game. We take turns picking up rubber ducks from a pool. We count how many ducks we pick up and describe their colors and patterns.

## Operation: Collect that Data

Let's collect quantitative and qualitative data. Can you count the ducks that William and Luca have? Who has more? Can you describe the different costumes the ducks are wearing?

43

After enjoying all the rides and games, our next stop is the concession stand. As we stand in line, we count all the different types of snacks and describe the sweet smells that fill the air.

## Operation: Collect that Data

Let's collect qualitative data!
Can you help William describe all the yummy foods?

After waiting 25 million hours, it's finally our turn to order! I choose a hot dog with ketchup, and Luca gets nachos with cheese. Mommy finds us a table, and we sit down to enjoy our yummy food.

## Operation: Collect that Data

Let's collect quantitative data! How many people are eating hot dogs? How many people are eating nachos? How many people are eating pizza? Which is the most popular?

After we finish our snack, Mommy stands up and gathers everyone's attention. "Attention, everyone! I have some exciting news to share. Our team of data detectives completed a very special mission! They explored different booths, collected data, and used their detective skills to learn about two data types." Wow. Did we really do it?

"I am so proud of each of you," Mommy says. "You leveraged the power of data to answer questions, make important decisions, and solve big problems. Well done, data detectives!" Mommy then gives us our Data Detective badges and certificates. The crowd bursts into cheers and applause, making us feel super good.

When I get back to the car, I let out a big yawn. I am so excited, but also very tired. "Aaaah." Is this why grown-up data detectives drink coffee during their missions? As I close my eyes, I start dreaming about our next exciting adventure. Hmm... I wonder what my next mission will be?

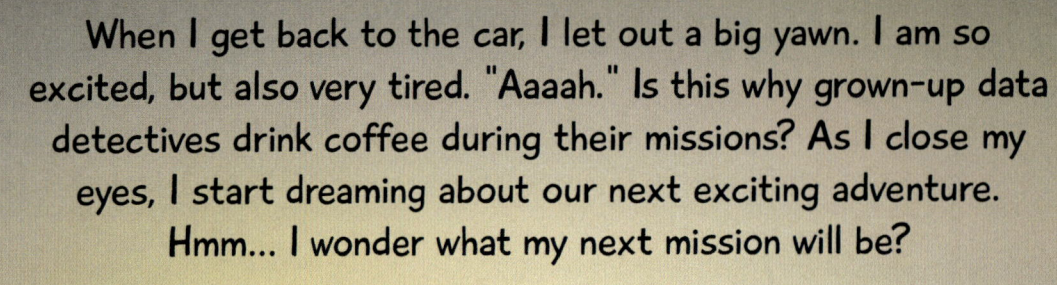

# The Data Detective

## Certificate of Achievement

This hereby certifies _____ has successfully completed the __Carnival__ mission and has learned to collect quantitative and qualitative data on this ____ day of _____.

*William*

Author, The Data Detective

## Operation: Find Those Tickets

Data Detective, before we went to the carnival, I secretly hid 23 tickets from Mommy. Can you find the 23 tickets I hid from Mommy before she does? I will give you a little hint—there is one in my bedroom. Let's see if you can find them all! Ready, set, go!

Grown-up Detectives: Let your Data Detectives know how long it took you to find the tickets and see if they can beat your time!

Scan the code for more missions, exclusive merch, and to stay updated on my journey to become a data detective.

https://thedatadetective.org/

Made in the USA
Middletown, DE
11 March 2025

72212288R00036